# Financial Risk Management:

# A Simple Introduction

*Also by K.H. Erickson*

## <u>Simple Introductions</u>

Accounting and Finance Formulas
Choice Theory
Corporate Finance Formulas
eBay
Econometrics
Financial Economics
Financial Risk Management
Game Theory
Game Theory for Business
Investment Appraisal
Marketing Management Concepts and Tools
Mathematical Formulas for Economics and Business
Microeconomics

# Financial Risk Management:

## A Simple Introduction

K.H. Erickson

# Contents

# 1 Introduction

Individuals, businesses, corporations, and governments are always searching for profitable investment opportunities which can offer an increased return. But the potential for a greater return will typically go hand in hand with greater risk, and there's a danger than an investment strategy can backfire and end up costing more than it creates. Risk can come in many forms and while much risk can be avoided with well researched investments, or eliminated with a diversified portfolio, a degree of unavoidable market risk will always remain and therefore effective financial risk management is a central part of any investment strategy.

One of the most significant elements of market risk is interest rate risk, as changing yield rates can reduce the value of an asset or portfolio, and interest rate risk is a focus of this book. The field of financial risk management is explored in depth using theory, formulas, calculations, and examples, and then applied to the case study of the 1994 Orange County, California bankruptcy to examine whether the financial failure could have been avoided. Basic prior knowledge of derivatives and econometrics is assumed and used in the analysis.

Financial risk management involves first determining the risk exposure of an investment or portfolio, and this is explored using leverage, duration, modified duration, convexity, effective duration and effective convexity. Value at risk (VaR) is the next focus, and the three main variance-covariance, historical simulation, and Monte Carlo methods are explained and compared, along with the related square root of time rule. Detailed steps to calculate the variance-covariance, historical simulation, and Monte Carlo value at risk in Excel are provided. An exponentially weighted moving average (EWMA) is then introduced to predict factor change, interest rate or return volatility, and simple steps to calculate the EWMA and backtest the data for reliability in Excel are presented.

An extended empirical case study for Orange County's bankruptcy in 1994 takes up the remainder of the book. First the history of how the situation came to pass is explained, with Orange County's balance sheet, leverage, duration, effective duration, and modified duration examined to determine the extent of the county's risk exposure, and assess whether the bankruptcy was inevitable or if alternatives were available. This discussion is then built upon with detailed value at risk and EWMA analysis as the potential for risk management is debated. The final section looks into theoretical hedging strategies for Orange County, examining a range of financial derivatives and how they may be used to hedge interest rate risk.

# 2 Financial Risk Exposure

## 2.1 Debt and Leverage

The level of debt held, known as the leverage, is a key factor affecting the risk exposure of an investor. Greater debt levels increase risk exposure as debt involves interest payments to the creditors who issued it, which must be paid before other commitments can be funded, and if interest rates change then greater repayments may be owed by an investor. This type of risk is known as interest rate risk, and an investor may be able to avoid it on a fixed repayment plan for small amounts of debt, but for large amounts of debt such as with mortgages the repayment costs will depend on the level of interest rates.

An investor's balance sheet can be examined to calculate their leverage, and leverage is the ratio of all liabilities to non-debt liabilities (i.e. shareholders' equity). It can be found by dividing the total value of all liabilities by the total value of all non-debt liabilities:

Leverage = Total liabilities / Non-debt liabilities
Leverage = Total liabilities / Shareholders' equity

If an investor has no debt at all then debt liability value will be zero, and non-debt liability value = total liability value. This simplifies the equation to that below:

### *An investor without debt*

Leverage = Total liabilities / Non-debt liabilities
Leverage = Total liabilities / Total liabilities
Leverage = 1

The case of an investor without debt or interest rate risk, with a leverage level of 1, is used as a basis to evaluate situations where an investor does have debt and risk exposure to interest rate risk. The higher the leverage factor moves above 1 the greater the risk factor an investor will face.

For example, an investor's total liabilities may come to £100 million, of which £80 million may relate to shareholder's equity and £20 million to mortgage debt obligations. In this example the investor's leverage is 1.25:

### *An investor with debt*

Leverage = Total liabilities / Non-debt liabilities
Leverage = Total liabilities / Shareholders' equity
Leverage = £100 million / £80 million
Leverage = 1.25

Alternatively, an investor may hold liabilities to the total value of £900,000, with £400,000 as mortgage costs, and £500,000 as investor's equity. If shares are not publicly distributed to shareholders (i.e. with a private firm) then shareholders' equity equals investor's equity, and here this gives a leverage factor of 1.8:

Leverage = Total liabilities / Non-debt liabilities
Leverage = Total liabilities / Shareholders' equity
Leverage = £900,000 / £500,000
Leverage = 1.8

There is no such thing as leverage which is too high or too low, and it all depends on the firm's preferences. Greater debt and leverage will increase an investor's interest rate risk, and see interest rate changes cause larger changes to the level of interest payments they must pay on their debt and to portfolio value, but this can work both ways. Increased interest rate risk is a bad thing if interest rates go in an unwanted direction and reduce the value of portfolio securities, but a good thing if interest rates go in the desired direction and raise the value of portfolio securities.

## 2.2 Duration

(Macaulay) duration measures the average length of time a bond holder must wait before receiving cash payments, as the average of all payments weighted by discounted cash flow present value. A higher duration naturally means greater risk exposure, as there is more time for something to happen which changes expected cash flows.

Finding duration requires 6 areas of information (Reilly and Brown, 2008). The first three are: 1) the yield to maturity (YTM); 2) the cash flow (CF) received for the year; 3) the number of years into the future (N) the cash flow will be received, assuming annual payments. The remaining factors require calculation: 4) the present value (PV) of the year's cash flow after discounting with the yield rate due to the time value of money; 5) the cash flow present value for each year as a percentage (PV%) of the present value of the sum of all present value cash flows ($\sum$PV) (i.e. a bond's PV price); 6) each year's cash flow present value as a percentage of price multiplied by the number of years into the future the cash flow is received (PV% * N), where the sum of these values is the duration:

$$PV = CF / (1 + YTM)^N$$
$$PV\% = PV / \sum PV$$
$$Duration = \sum(PV\% * N)$$

As calculating duration is relatively complicated it can be more easily explained using some examples. Annual interest payments are assumed, and a yield to maturity (YTM) of 8% is used to determine the duration of two bonds, bond A and bond B, with the following features:

## Bond A

Face value: £1,000; Maturity: 3 years; Coupon: 4%

## Bond B

Face value: £1,000; Maturity: 3 years; Coupon: 9%

## Bond A

Looking first at bond A in depth, it's possible to calculate the values of CF (cash flow) for each of the 3 years until the bond reaches maturity. Each year will have a cash flow of 4% (the coupon rate) of the £1,000 face value of the bond, while the final year will also see the principal (face value) paid out as part of the cash flow. The CF values for bond A are:

$$\text{Year 1 CF} = 1,000 * 0.04$$
$$\text{Year 1 CF} = £40$$
$$\text{Year 2 CF} = 1,000 * 0.04$$

Year 2 CF = £40
Year 3 CF = 1,000 + (1,000 * 0.04)
Year 3 CF = £1,040

And with these numbers the PV (present value) of cash flows can then be found for bond A:

$$PV = CF / (1 + YTM)^N$$
PV of Year 1 CF = $40 / (1.08)^1$
PV of Year 1 CF = £37.04
PV of Year 2 CF = $40 / (1.08)^2$
PV of Year 2 CF = £34.29
PV of Year 3 CF = $1,040 / (1.08)^3$
PV of Year 3 CF = £825.59

From here the PV% can be found:

$$PV\% = PV / \sum PV$$
$\sum PV = 37.04 + 34.29 + 825.59$
$\sum PV = Price = £896.92$
PV% for Year 1 PV = 37.04 / 896.92
PV% for Year 1 PV = 0.0413
PV% for Year 2 PV = 34.29 / 896.92
PV% for Year 2 PV = 0.0382
PV% for Year 3 PV = 825.59 / 896.92
PV% for Year 3 PV = 0.9205

And then (PV% * N) can be calculated and summed to give the duration of bond A:

$$(PV\% * N) \text{ for Year } 1 = 0.0413 * 1$$
$$(PV\% * N) \text{ for Year } 1 = 0.0413$$
$$(PV\% * N) \text{ for Year } 2 = 0.0382 * 2$$
$$(PV\% * N) \text{ for Year } 2 = 0.0764$$
$$(PV\% * N) \text{ for Year } 3 = 0.9205 * 3$$
$$(PV\% * N) \text{ for Year } 3 = 2.7615$$

$$\text{Duration} = \sum(PV\% * N) = 0.0413 + 0.0764 + 2.7615$$
$$\text{Duration} = 2.88 \text{ years}$$

*Bond B*

Looking next at bond B, each of the 3 years until the bond reaches maturity will have a cash flow of 9% (the coupon rate) of the £1,000 face value of the bond, while the final year also sees the principal (face value) paid out as part of the cash flow. The CF values for bond B are:

$$\text{Year } 1 \text{ CF} = 1,000 * 0.09$$
$$\text{Year } 1 \text{ CF} = £90$$
$$\text{Year } 2 \text{ CF} = 1,000 * 0.09$$
$$\text{Year } 2 \text{ CF} = £90$$
$$\text{Year } 3 \text{ CF} = 1,000 + (1,000 * 0.09)$$
$$\text{Year } 3 \text{ CF} = £1,090$$

And the PV of cash flows for bond B are:

$$PV = CF / (1 + YTM)^N$$
$$\text{PV of Year 1 CF} = 90 / (1.08)^1$$
$$\text{PV of Year 1 CF} = £83.33$$
$$\text{PV of Year 2 CF} = 90 / (1.08)^2$$
$$\text{PV of Year 2 CF} = £77.16$$
$$\text{PV of Year 3 CF} = 1,090 / (1.08)^3$$
$$\text{PV of Year 3 CF} = £865.28$$

From here the PV% can be found:

$$PV\% = PV / \sum PV$$
$$\sum PV = 83.33 + 77.16 + 865.28$$
$$\sum PV = \text{Price} = £1,025.77$$
$$\text{PV\% for Year 1 PV} = 83.33 / 1,025.77$$
$$\text{PV\% for Year 1 PV} = 0.0812$$
$$\text{PV\% for Year 2 PV} = 77.16 / 1,025.77$$
$$\text{PV\% for Year 2 PV} = 0.0752$$
$$\text{PV\% for Year 3 PV} = 865.28 / 1,025.77$$
$$\text{PV\% for Year 3 PV} = 0.8435$$

And then (PV% * N) can be calculated and summed to give the duration of bond B:

$$(PV\% * N) \text{ for Year 1} = 0.0812 * 1$$
$$(PV\% * N) \text{ for Year 1} = 0.0812$$

$$(PV\% * N) \text{ for Year } 2 = 0.0752 * 2$$
$$(PV\% * N) \text{ for Year } 2 = 0.1504$$
$$(PV\% * N) \text{ for Year } 3 = 0.8435 * 3$$
$$(PV\% * N) \text{ for Year } 3 = 2.5305$$

$$\text{Duration} = \sum(PV\% * N) = 0.0812 + 0.1504 + 2.5305$$
$$\text{Duration} = 2.76 \text{ years}$$

These two example bonds reveal some of the notable characteristics of (Macaulay) duration. First, while a zero coupon bond such as a Treasury bill (T-bill) will have a duration equal to its maturity, the duration of a bond with coupon payments is always less than its term to maturity as duration weights interim interest payments. This is visible here with 2.88 years duration for bond A and 2.76 years duration for bond B compared to a maturity of 3 years for both bonds.

Second, there is a generally positive relationship between duration and term to maturity, and a bond with a longer term to maturity will almost always have a higher duration, but duration increases at a decreasing rate as the term to maturity is longer. The relationship is only general and not direct however, because as maturity increases the present value of the principal to be received at maturity at the end of a bond's life declines in value due to greater discounting, and this will reduce duration. This second characteristic is related to the first noted above, and if the duration of a bond with coupon payments is always less than its term to maturity it follows that a longer term to maturity enables a longer duration.

The third characteristic of duration is that there is an inverse relationship between coupon rate and duration, and a larger coupon ensures that a bond will have a shorter duration as a greater amount of total cash flows will come earlier in the bond's life as interest payments. This is shown with the two bonds here as bond B's 9% coupon has a duration of 2.76 and bond A's lower 4% coupon gives a longer duration of 2.88 years.

Finally, other things being equal, there is an inverse relationship between the yield to maturity (YTM) and duration. A higher yield to maturity reduces a bond's duration as it ensures greater discounting of far off cash flows relative to closer cash flows, to see cash flows received sooner play a greater role in average payments.

## 2.3 Modified Duration and Risk Sensitivity

As the duration measure describes how long on average a bond holder will have to wait before receiving income from their investments, it can also be used as the basis for a measure which gives the interest rate risk sensitivity of a bond over the time the holder waits for the investment income. And an understanding of an asset's risk sensitivity could support the ultimate goal of managing and removing risk. Modified duration ($D_M$) can be used to show a bond's risk sensitivity, and it is calculated using duration, the relevant interest rate (i) which equals a bond's yield to maturity (YTM), and the no. of payments (m) made per year with discrete (non-continuous) compounding:

$$\text{Modified duration } (D_M) = \text{Duration} / (1 + i / m)$$

The details for bond A in the last section can be used as an example, and the duration for bond A was 2.88 years, and the yield to maturity was 8% with one payment per year. Modified duration is then calculated as follows:

$$\text{Modified duration } (D_M) = 2.88 / (1 + 0.08 / 1)$$
$$D_M = 2.88 / 1.08$$
$$D_M = 2.67$$

The modified duration measure makes it possible to immunize a portfolio against interest rate risk over a holding period, and this process ensures that the value of a bond portfolio at the end of the holding period is at least as much with any pattern of interest rates as it would be with constant interest rates. If any changes in interest rates are seen as equivalent for all bond maturities (i.e. parallel shifts in the relationship between maturity and yield, on the yield curve), then a portfolio is immunized if modified duration always equals the remaining time horizon of the investment. This works because duration is the time period where profits and losses, and price and reinvestment risk, are balanced. In practice however yield curve shifts may face random shocks which can ruin the bond immunization process. But this can be resolved with the bulleting of assets where securities have a range of duration levels, and for example, a portfolio with an investment horizon of five years would contain four to six year duration securities to cover the effects of random shocks to the yield curve. Another method to manage shocks is duration matching, where the duration of a portfolio's assets is matched against the duration of a portfolio's liabilities.

To use modified duration to immunize a bond portfolio the precise effect of interest rate changes on bond value and price changes (which in turn change duration) must be known, so an investor can take on other positions which balance the risk and counteract the effects of interest rate changes in one direction. But as modified duration is the sum of discounted cash flows divided by price it can be used to estimate bond changes.

The formula below shows the estimated percentage change in a bond portfolio's price (%$\Delta$P) to be equal to the negative (–) of modified duration ($D_M$) multiplied by the percentage change in interest rates or yield (%$\Delta$Y):

$D_M$ estimated % price change: %$\Delta$P = $-D_M$ * %$\Delta$Y

Bond A's modified duration was calculated at 2.67, and in a scenario where the yield to maturity fell with a percentage change in yield of –1.5% modified duration's estimate of the percentage change in bond A's price is:

$D_M$ estimated % price change: %$\Delta$P = $-D_M$ * %$\Delta$Y
$D_M$ estimated % price change: %$\Delta$P = $-2.67$ * $-0.015$
$D_M$ estimated % price change: %$\Delta$P = $0.04005$

This +4.005% percentage price change estimation using duration would then be multiplied by the original bond price before the change in yield had occurred, to give the numerical modified duration estimate of the price change. And that estimate would be added to the original price to predict the new bond portfolio price after the yield change:

$D_M$ estimated price change: $\Delta P$ = Bond portfolio price *
$D_M$ estimated % price change
New bond portfolio price = $D_M$ estimated price change +
Bond portfolio price

For example, bond A's price was £896.92 and the modified duration estimate of the percentage change in price after a −1.5% yield change was +4.005%:

$D_M$ estimated price change: $\Delta P$ = Bond portfolio price *
$D_M$ estimated % price change
$D_M$ estimated price change = 896.92 * 0.04005
$D_M$ estimated price change = 35.92

New bond portfolio price = $D_M$ estimated price change +
Bond portfolio price
New bond portfolio price = 35.92 + 896.92
New bond portfolio price = £932.84

However, this formula isn't exact, only approximating the true relationship between yield changes and portfolio price known as the price-yield curve. Modified duration assumes that the price-yield curve is linear (a straight line) but it is actually convex. This causes a disparity between the predictions made by modified duration and the actual impact of yield changes on bond price, as the following price-yield curve diagram suggests (Fabozzi et al., 2005).

# Price-yield curve

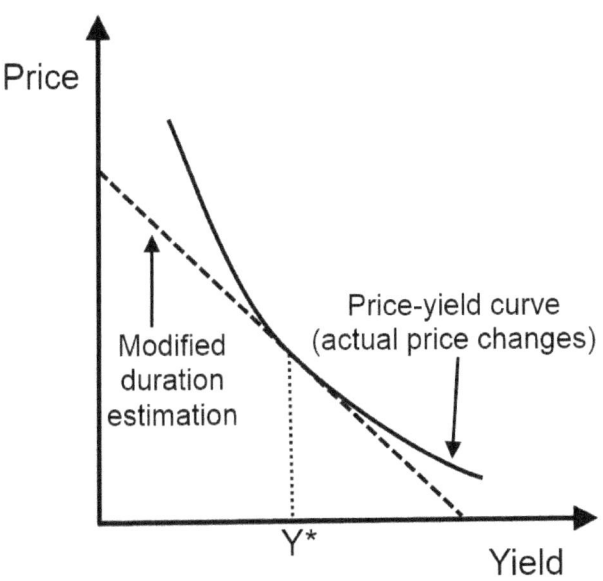

The starting interest rate and yield is point Y*, and for small yield rises or falls away from this point modified duration's estimation of portfolio price changes (the dashed line) may equal the actual price changes on the price-yield curve, but for large interest rate changes modified duration's estimation will be increasingly inaccurate to the extent of a bond's convexity and curvature. Note from the diagram that the convexity of the yield curve is not even, and a yield rise will cause a smaller decrease in price than an equivalent yield fall will cause an increase in price.

Modified duration's estimation will underestimate price increases for interest rate falls, and overestimate price decreases for interest rate rises. This inaccuracy makes bond immunization more difficult, and using modified duration to forecast potential bond price changes and immunize a portfolio against interest rate risk may work well with small interest rate changes, but only have a limited effect with larger interest rate changes. To forecast bond price changes more accurately, and to enable full immunization of a portfolio against interest rate risk in situations with large changes in yield, the effects of a bond's convexity must also be included in the analysis. This is the subject of the next section.

## 2.4 Convexity

The addition of convexity into the analysis will see bond price predictions accurately account for both the risk and risk sensitivity facing portfolio assets. Convexity (C) shows changes in duration, and mathematically it is the second derivative of price with respect to the yield (interest rate). Convexity can be found as follows:

$$\text{Convexity} = (d^2P \,/\, di^2) \,/\, \text{Price}$$
$$d^2P \,/\, di^2 = 1 \,/\, (1 + i)^2 \left[ \sum (N^2 + N) \, CF_N \,/\, (1 + i)^N \right]$$

N here is the number of years until a cash flow (CF) is received, i is the interest rate and yield to maturity. Calculation of convexity involves a similar process to that for duration, with one modification and two additional steps. Example calculations of convexity will return to the two sample bonds from earlier, bond A and bond B, with an 8% yield to maturity again assumed.

### *Bond A*

Face value: £1,000; Maturity: 3 years; Coupon: 4%

Bond A's cash flow present value (PV) for each year and in total has already been calculated at:

PV of Year 1 CF = £37.04
PV of Year 2 CF = £34.29
PV of Year 3 CF = £825.59
$\sum$PV = Price = £896.92

Each year's PV is then multiplied by $(N^2 + N)$ and the summation noted.

$[PV * (N^2 + N)]$ for Year 1 = 37.04 * 2
$[PV * (N^2 + N)]$ for Year 1 = £74.08
$[PV * (N^2 + N)]$ for Year 2 = 34.29 * 6
$[PV * (N^2 + N)]$ for Year 2 = £205.74
$[PV * (N^2 + N)]$ for Year 3 = 825.59 * 12
$[PV * (N^2 + N)]$ for Year 3 = £9,907.08
$\sum[PV * (N^2 + N)]$ = 74.08 + 205.74 + 9,907.08
$\sum[PV * (N^2 + N)]$ = £10,186.90

$\sum[PV * (N^2 + N)] = [\sum (N^2 + N) CF_N / (1 + i)^N]$
$[\sum (N^2 + N) CF_N / (1 + i)^N]$ = £10,186.90

To find the $d^2P / di^2$ value which represents half of the convexity equation this value is multiplied by $1 / (1 + i)^2$:

$1 / (1 + i)^2 = 1 / (1 + 0.08)^2$
$1 / (1 + i)^2 = 0.8573$

This is then put back into the convexity equation:

$$d^2P / di^2 = 1 / (1 + i)^2 \left[ \sum (N^2 + N)\, CF_N / (1 + i)^N \right]$$
$$d^2P / di^2 = 0.8573\,[10{,}186.90]$$
$$d^2P / di^2 = 8{,}733.23$$

$$\text{Convexity} = (d^2P / di^2) / \text{Price}$$
$$\text{Convexity} = 8{,}733.23 / 896.92$$
$$\text{Convexity} = 9.737$$

The same process can then be calculated for bond B:

## Bond B

Face value: £1,000; Maturity: 3 years; Coupon: 9%

PV of Year 1 CF = £83.33
PV of Year 2 CF = £77.16
PV of Year 3 CF = £865.28
$\sum$PV = Price = £1,025.77

$[PV * (N^2 + N)]$ for Year 1 = 83.33 * 2
$[PV * (N^2 + N)]$ for Year 1 = £166.66
$[PV * (N^2 + N)]$ for Year 2 = 77.16 * 6
$[PV * (N^2 + N)]$ for Year 2 = £462.96
$[PV * (N^2 + N)]$ for Year 3 = 865.28 * 12
$[PV * (N^2 + N)]$ for Year 3 = £10,383.36
$\sum[PV * (N^2 + N)] = 166.66 + 462.96 + 10{,}383.36$
$\sum[PV * (N^2 + N)] = £11{,}012.98$

$$[\sum (N^2 + N)\, CF_N / (1 + i)^N] = £11{,}012.98$$
$$1 / (1 + i)^2 = 0.8573$$

$$d^2P / di^2 = 1 / (1 + i)^2\, [\sum (N^2 + N)\, CF_N / (1 + i)^N]$$
$$d^2P / di^2 = 0.8573\, [11{,}012.98]$$
$$d^2P / di^2 = £9{,}441.43$$

$$\text{Convexity} = (d^2P / di^2) / \text{Price}$$
$$\text{Convexity} = 9{,}441.43 / 1{,}025.77$$
$$\text{Convexity} = 9{,}441.43 / 1{,}025.77$$
$$\text{Convexity} = 9.204$$

The estimate of bond price changes based on convexity equals 0.5 multiplied by convexity value (C), multiplied by percentage change in yield squared $(\%\Delta Y)^2$, multiplied by bond portfolio price:

$$\text{Convexity estimated price change} = 0.5 * C * (\%\Delta Y)^2 *$$
$$\text{Bond portfolio price}$$

The convexity estimate of the price change is added to the original bond price and modified duration estimate of the price change, to give the complete estimate for a bond portfolio's new price following a change in yield:

$$\text{New bond price} = \text{Bond price} + D_M \text{ estimated price change}$$
$$+ \text{Convexity estimated price change}$$

For example, assuming the same −1.5% change in yield used earlier, and bond A's price of 896.92, and convexity of 9.737 the formula gives the following result:

$$\text{Convexity estimated price change} = 0.5 * C * (\%\Delta Y)^2 * \text{Bond portfolio price}$$

$$\text{Convexity estimated price change} = 0.5 * 9.737 * (-0.015)^2 * 896.92$$

$$\text{Convexity estimate of price change} = 0.98$$

Combining this value with the calculated duration result gives a more accurate new bond price:

$$\text{New bond price} = \text{Bond price} + D_M \text{ estimated price change} + \text{Convexity estimated price change}$$

$$\text{New bond price} = 896.92 + 35.92 + 0.98$$

$$\text{New bond price} = £933.82$$

And combining all of the above steps is a quick way to calculate the new bond portfolio price after a yield change:

$$\text{New bond price} = \text{Bond price} + (\text{Bond price} * -D_M * \%\Delta Y) + (0.5 * \text{Bond price} * C * \%\Delta Y^2)$$

Although combining duration and convexity estimates can give an accurate estimation of bond portfolio price changes following changes in interest rates, there are flaws with the method. Fooladi and Roberts (2000) note that duration analysis can ignore default risk for bonds, where debt obligations are not met. A default would mean that the calculated duration will be inaccurate, and actual duration may be less if cash was received before the default occurred, or more if cash was promised and interest paid after the default. With bonds containing default risk the duration measure will therefore not be a fully accurate measure of the interest rate risk sensitivity. Broadening this discussion out from individual bonds to a portfolio, any leveraged portfolio will have default risk as there's the risk that debt payments may not be met and assets seized as collateral in response, and therefore duration values, and the modified duration and convexity values derived from them, are not completely reliable in a portfolio with debt.

Duration is also inaccurate with certain specific types of non-standard or 'non-vanilla' bonds, such as bonds with embedded options. With these bonds it's more accurate to use effective duration and effective convexity measures and the next section explains these additional measures further.

## 2.5 Effective Duration and Effective Convexity

While (Macaulay) duration and modified duration are useful measures to predict the effects of interest rate changes on price they have three significant limitations. The first of these, that they are inaccurate with large yield changes, has already been noted and can be addressed with the addition of convexity. But duration and convexity can't accurately represent assets with embedded options, especially call options where a buyer has the right but not the obligation to buy a certain amount of a particular asset at a given time and price, nor assets affected by factors beyond interest rates such as common stocks or real estate. To overcome these issues duration and convexity can be replaced with effective duration and effective convexity, which directly measure the interest rate sensitivity of an asset and use a pricing model to estimate market prices after an interest rate change.

The formulas for effective duration ($D_E$) and effective convexity ($C_E$) are based around the current asset price before any yield change (P), the estimated price of an asset after a downward shift in yield (P⁻), the estimated price of an asset after an upward shift in yield (P⁺), and the assumed size of the yield shift (S) in basis points (i.e. 1 / 10,000 or 1 / 100 of 1%):

31

$$\text{Effective Duration } (D_E) = (P^- - P^+) / (2 * P * S)$$
$$\text{Effective Convexity } (C_E) = (P^- + P^+ - 2P) / (P * S^2)$$

The example bond A will again be revisited to show how these measures are calculated, and it has the following features:

## *Bond A*

Face value: £1,000; Maturity: 3 years; Coupon: 4%; Initial yield to maturity: 8%; Price: £896.92

Assuming a change in yield of 100 basis points or 1% would give the following stats to be used in the effective duration and effective convexity formulas:

$$S = 0.01; P = 896.92; P^- = 921.27; P^+ = 873.44$$

$P^-$ and $P^+$ price values were found using the present value (PV) formula first explained in the duration section. $P^-$ is the sum of cash flow present values for bond A, $\sum PV$ = Price, assuming a yield to maturity (YTM) of 7%, and $P^+$ is the $\sum PV$ = Price with a YTM of 9%.

$$\text{Effective Duration } (D_E) = (P^- - P^+) / (2 * P * S)$$
$$D_E = (921.27 - 873.44) / (2 * 896.92 * 0.01)$$
$$D_E = 2.67$$

$$\text{Effective Convexity } (C_E) = (P^- + P^+ - 2P) / (P * S^2)$$
$$C_E = (921.27 + 873.44 - (2*896.92)) / (896.92*0.01^2)$$
$$C_E = 9.7$$

The effective duration value of 2.67 and effective convexity value of 9.7 are similar to bond A's original duration of 2.88 and convexity of 9.737, only a little lower. But this pattern will be not necessarily be the case with non-vanilla bonds with embedded options, and effective duration can actually be greater than maturity. There is also the potential for effective duration or effective convexity to be negative.

Although a useful measure to address the limitations of duration and convexity it may not always be possible to use effective duration or effective convexity, as the exact effects of interest rate changes on price can often be hard to acquire. One way to overcome this is with empirical duration, which is an asset's actual percentage price change after a yield change during a specific historical period. But even empirical duration may be hard to apply for a portfolio containing a diverse range of assets, some of which may be relatively new and have a limited history.

With a leveraged portfolio involving debt payments the effect of a yield change on the portfolio price may also be hard to determine, but in this case the effective duration measure above can be replaced with a simpler version. Multiplying duration by leverage gives another type of effective duration, which can be used as a proxy to note proportional changes in a bond's price given a change in interest rates. It accounts for bonds with uncertain cash flows and debt obligations which affect portfolio value:

$$\text{Effective duration} = \text{Duration} * \text{Leverage}$$

For example, if a portfolio's duration was 3 years, and its leverage factor was 1.2, then effective duration equals:

$$\text{Effective duration} = \text{Duration} * \text{Leverage}$$
$$\text{Effective duration} = 3 * 1.2$$
$$\text{Effective duration} = 3.6 \text{ years}$$

The figures in this example and a leverage factor of 1.2 suggest that the bond holder won't have to wait 3 years on average before receiving cash payments but more like 3.6 years, due to the debt and interest payment obligations, and this is a significant difference. With a leveraged portfolio the effective duration measure will be more accurate than the (Macaulay) duration measure in revealing an investor's risk exposure, and it should therefore be calculated and taken into consideration.

# 3 Value at Risk

## 3.1 Value at Risk Defined

While it's useful to know a portfolio's risk exposure and the risk sensitivity of prices to interest rate changes, it's often difficult to act on these factors alone. To prepare a detailed financial risk management strategy an investor needs to know the precise amount of money that is at risk, and what they stand to lose in various scenarios. The widely used Value at Risk (VaR) risk measure can provide an answer to this question and it represents the maximum possible loss in portfolio value over a period, and VaR essentially measures the downside risk in a portfolio. However, the VaR is never a certainty and is always associated with a specific confidence level only, leaving a given probability that the calculated VaR value can be exceeded over the next period of choice, whether a day, month or a year.

For example, the VaR result may find that a firm has a monthly value at risk of £10,900 at the 95% confidence level. This would mean that there is a 95% likelihood that the firm will lose no more than £10,900 from the portfolio value over the next month, and a 5% chance (100% – 95%

= 5%) that the firm in question could lose more than £10,900 over the following month. Alternatively a portfolio's annual value at risk may be $25.5 million at the 99% confidence level, and this means that there is a 99% chance that they'll lose no more than $25.5 million over the next year, and a 1% (100% – 99% = 1%) chance that a portfolio may lose more than $25.5 million over the next year.

There are three different methods commonly used to calculate the value at risk. The *variance-covariance* method assumes that underlying factors have a normal distribution (mathematically this is zero skewness, for perfect symmetry, and a kurtosis of three, to define the peakedness and spread of the distribution), and that changes in portfolio value are a linear function of changes in factors, and that the latter causes the former. The *historical simulation* method takes the current portfolio and exposes it to historical changes in market factors. And the *Monte Carlo simulation* method takes the current portfolio and exposes it to randomly generated changes in market factors (Linsmeier and Pearson, 2000). The following sections examine each of these three methods in depth.

## 3.2 Variance-Covariance Method

The variance-covariance method to calculate value at risk (VaR) at a chosen confidence level for a single asset follows the formula:

*Variance-covariance VaR for 1 asset*

VaR = Asset value * Asset volatility * CV

The asset value is its price; asset volatility is the standard deviation (SD) of an asset's daily or monthly etc. returns chosen as the data sample; and CV is the critical value at the chosen percentage confidence level in the statistical t-tables. A 95% confidence level is usually chosen, and any lower than this is thought to allow too much room for error in results, while a more stringent confidence level above 95% is often thought to give too much weight to highly unlikely or very rare occurrences. The critical value from the statistical t-table distribution at the 95% confidence level (equals a 5% significance level for 5% margin of error) for large samples is 1.65. This means that there is a 95% probability that the observation will be less than 1.65 standard deviations from the mean observation value (assuming a normal distribution of data), and a 5% probability that the observation will be 1.65 or more standard deviations from the mean. As a 95% confidence level is typically chosen for statistical analysis the 1.65 value is a common feature in many value at risk formulas.

For example, an asset's current price (value) may be £120, and the volatility (SD) of its returns may be 20%:

$$VaR = Asset\ value * Asset\ volatility * CV$$
$$VaR = 120 * 0.2 * 1.65$$
$$VaR = £39.60$$

The value at risk for the asset holder here is therefore £39.60 at the 95% confidence level and 5% margin of error (significance level), and if daily returns were used to determine the asset's volatility this would the daily VaR, while if monthly returns had been used to find the asset's volatility then £39.60 would be the monthly VaR. If daily returns were used then on 19 days out of every 20 (95%) the asset holder can be confident they would lose no more than the £39.60 daily VaR, but on every 1 day out of 20 (5%) the asset holder can be expected to suffer a loss greater than the £39.60 daily VaR.

However, the VaR formula given above is only for a single asset, and in a portfolio a different formula will be required. The asset price can be easily replaced with a portfolio price (portfolio value), and the 1.65 critical value will remain for a 95% confidence level test, but the asset volatility will need to be replaced with a portfolio volatility. In a two asset portfolio the volatility (standard deviation, SD) of each asset must be weighted by the proportion the asset represents in the portfolio, and the combined effect of the two assets must also be noted if there is correlation between them. The volatility of a two asset portfolio can be found using two formulas one after the other:

*Variance (SD²) and volatility (SD) for 2 asset portfolio*

$$SD^2 = P_1{}^2*SD_1{}^2 + P_2{}^2*SD_2{}^2 + 2*P_1*P_2*C_{12}*SD_1*SD_2$$
$$SD = \sqrt{SD^2}$$

In the first formula for portfolio variance here $SD_1$ and $SD_2$ are the standard deviation values (volatility of returns) for assets 1 and 2 respectively, while $P_1$ and $P_2$ are the proportions each asset takes up in the portfolio, and $C_{12}$ is the correlation between asset 1 and asset 2. Taking the square root ($\sqrt{}$) of the portfolio variance gives the portfolio volatility.

For example, asset 1 may have a standard deviation of 6% and represent a 25% proportion of the portfolio, while asset 2 may have a standard deviation of returns of 10% and take up a 75% proportion of the portfolio. The correlation coefficient for asset 1 and asset 2 may be -24%, and a rise in one asset's returns may see the other's returns fall by 24%. These values give a portfolio standard deviation or volatility as follows:

$$SD^2 = P_1^2*SD_1^2 + P_2^2*SD_2^2 + 2*P_1*P_2*C_{12}*SD_1*SD_2$$
$$SD^2 = (0.25^2*0.06^2) + (0.75^2*0.1^2) + (2*0.25*0.75*(-0.24)$$
$$*0.06*0.1)$$
$$SD^2 = 0.63806$$
$$SD = 0.7988$$

This value would then be put back into the VaR formula for a portfolio, and if the portfolio price was for example £119 million the VaR would be:

### *Variance-covariance VaR for portfolio*

$$VaR = Portfolio\ value * Portfolio\ volatility * CV$$
$$VaR = 119 * 0.7988 * 1.65$$
$$VaR = £156.84\ million$$

£156.84 million would be the monthly value at risk level if monthly returns were used to calculate asset and portfolio volatility. This means that there would be a 95% likelihood that the maximum amount of money a firm could lose over the next month was £156.84 million, and a 5% chance that they could lose more than this (as a 95% confidence level and 5% significance level was chosen and the corresponding 1.65 critical value used in the formula). If daily returns had been used to find volatility then the analysis would concern the next day and not the next month.

For portfolios of three assets or more the two asset variance formula given here ($SD^2$) would be modified accordingly. Each additional asset's variance would be weighted by its proportion in the portfolio, and additional cross-product terms would be included to note the different relationships between the different pairs of assets.

With the formula for the variance-covariance VaR noted all that is left to do is to know how to calculate the relevant standard deviation, weighting, and correlation values. The weighting values are simple to calculate, and if the total portfolio value was £50 million and asset 1 had a value of £20 million, with asset 2 holding a value of £30 million, then asset 1 has a 20/50 = 0.4 weighting and asset 2 has a 30/50 = 0.6 weighting in the portfolio variance formula. Correlation values for the VaR formula depend on an asset's returns, and analysing the relationship between the returns of two different assets reveals their correlation, which may be either positive or negative.

As a simplifying assumption (when other information isn't available) returns for a bond or portfolio of bonds can be seen as the same as interest rate yield changes, as a change in interest rates may cause an equivalent movement in bond returns. Standard deviation values for the VaR formula would therefore be the standard deviation or volatility of interest rate yield changes. As the interest rate changes will be the same for all bonds in a bond portfolio the standard deviation (of interest rate changes) will also be the same for all bonds, and the correlation between portfolio assets will equal 1 to show perfect correlation between portfolio assets. This simplifies the variance formula for a portfolio and removes the need to account for separate standard deviation values, weightings, and correlation, and only a single standard deviation value would need to be put into the VaR formula. For example, if a bond portfolio was worth £5,000 and the standard deviation of interest rate changes was 12%, the 95% confidence level value at risk would be:

$$VaR = \text{Portfolio value} * \text{Portfolio volatility} * CV$$
$$VaR = 5,000 * 0.12 * 1.65$$
$$VaR = £990$$

However, if there were assets other than bonds in a portfolio, such as cash (which has zero standard deviation and is unaffected by interest rate changes) for example, then the bonds' proportion in the portfolio would have to be noted and weighted. For example, if a portfolio had a value of £30 million, containing £28.8 million of bonds and £1.2 million of cash, and the volatility of interest rates was 17%, then the standard deviation or volatility of overall portfolio returns would be:

Portfolio volatility = Bond volatility * Weight of bonds in portfolio
Portfolio volatility = 0.17 * (28.8/30)
Portfolio volatility = 0.17 * 0.96
Portfolio volatility = 0.1632

This value would then be put into the VaR formula:

VaR = Portfolio value * Portfolio volatility * CV
VaR = 30 * 0.1632 * 1.65
VaR = £8.078 million

This completes the theory of how to calculate VaR with the variance-covariance method, and specific details of how to calculate the VaR in practice with Excel are:

*Calculating variance-covariance VaR in Excel*

1). Collect interest rate data (for a bond portfolio) or price data (for a stock portfolio), using monthly data for longer time periods and daily or weekly interest rate data for shorter time periods. This can be done using DataStream or a similar service, and the time series data values can be downloaded into Excel in column B;

2). Create a new column in Excel which divides each and every interest rate data or price value by 100 to turn them into decimal (percentage) form. For example, if the

43

data values were in column B starting in B2 then in cell C2 you would type '=B2/100', and then move the cursor to the bottom right of the cell and click the small '+' symbol that appears to apply this formula to the entire column;

3). Create a new column in Excel which gives the change between each value and the previous one, to reveal the returns. If using price data which isn't continuously compounded (i.e. percentage changes) then, with the decimal price data values in column C, in cell D3 type '=(C3-C2)/C2', and apply this formula to the whole D column. If price data is continuously compounded (i.e. periodic returns) then the formula format for column D would be '=LN(C3/C2)' instead. And if using interest data where actual data values matter then the formula would only use subtraction to calculate the yield changes and returns, and the D column formula would be '=C3-C2';

4). Next the standard deviation of the interest rate or price changes is calculated by selecting all of the values and using Excel's STDEV function. For example, if there were one hundred changes for interest rates or prices in cells D3 to D102 then find an empty blank cell in excel and type '=STDEV(D3:102)';

5). Next determine the weightings of the different types of assets based on the proportion of the portfolio value they represent. If a purely bond portfolio this is not necessary as all bonds will be assumed to have the same standard deviation based on interest rates (unless additional information is available). In a bond and cash portfolio or asset portfolio this step is required however;

6). If a bond portfolio, or bond and cash portfolio, the final step is to multiply the portfolio value by any bonds relative to cash weighting, multiplied by the standard deviation of interest rate changes, multiplied by 1.65 (for a 95% confidence level). This gives the monthly value at risk (VaR) if monthly interest rate data was used, or daily VaR if daily interest rate yield data was used.

If the portfolio's assets were stocks, or bonds and stocks, then individual standard deviation values and weightings must be put into the portfolio variance formula with a calculated correlation value. To find the correlation between different assets first arrange the different returns (from changes in different prices, or changes in different prices and in interest rates if a stock and bonds portfolio) next to each other in columns. Then use Excel's 'Data', 'Data Analysis', 'Correlation' option and select all return values from the columns for the input range, and select OK (Analysis Toolpak may need to be added as an Add-in if not already there). This gives the correlation value and with the weighting and standard deviation values the portfolio variance and then volatility (standard deviation) can then be found using the two formulas already provided. Multiplying the portfolio standard deviation by the portfolio value, multiplied by 1.65 (for a 95% confidence level test) gives the variance-covariance VaR.

## 3.3 Historical Simulation

The historical simulation method of finding the value at risk (VaR) at a chosen significance level follows the formula:

*Historical simulation VaR for a portfolio*

VaR = Significance level percentile value for sorted values of (Portfolio value * Returns)

First, the returns (e.g. interest rate changes or price changes using an extended collection of historic interest rate or price data) must be calculated as explained in the last section. Then each and every one of these values is multiplied by the total value of the portfolio. Next the (returns by portfolio value) data column is sorted into ascending order from the lowest value to the highest, and then the value of the percentile of the chosen significance level is taken to give the value at risk (VaR). For example, with the commonly used 95% confidence level (95% chance the amount of value lost over a period will be equal to or lower than the calculated VaR), also known as the 5% significance level (5% chance that the amount of value lost will actually be higher than the calculated VaR), the relevant percentile for the VaR test would be 5%.

The specific steps to calculate the VaR in Excel using the historical simulation method are as follows:

## *Calculating historical simulation VaR in Excel*

1). Collect interest rate data or price data over an extended period using DataStream or similar, and download the data into Excel;

2). Create a new column in Excel which divides each and every interest rate data value or price value by 100;

3). Create another column in Excel which calculates the returns for the price or interest rate data, as explained above for the variance-covariance method;

4). Add a new column in Excel which multiplies each returns data value by the overall value of the portfolio;

5). Note where the 'returns multiplied by portfolio value' data values begin and end in the Excel cells, for example if the first value is in cell H3 and the last in H102 then the data range would be 'H3:H102'. Next find a blank cell in Excel and enter the relevant formula as follows: '=PERCENTILE(H3:H102,0.05)' where 'H3:H102' is the range of 'returns multiplied by portfolio value' data values, and 0.05 is the percentage margin of error in the VaR test, e.g. 95% confidence level = 5% or 0.05 margin of error. This gives the relevant value at risk, and if daily returns were used it will be the daily VaR, while if monthly returns were used it will be a monthly VaR.

## 3.4 Monte Carlo Simulation

The Monte Carlo simulation method of value at risk calculation is named after the famous casino area Monte Carlo in Monaco, and the method shares many similarities with casino gambling. Finding the Monte Carlo value at risk (VaR) at a chosen significance level uses the formula:

*Monte Carlo simulation VaR for a portfolio*

VaR = Significance level percentile value for sorted values of (Portfolio value * Randomly generated values)

Monte Carlo simulation generates data values as uniform random numbers between 0 and 1 are created in place of using historical values. And as the generated numbers are designed to be symmetric, and with a mean of 0 and a standard deviation of 1, they have three key features of a normal distribution and can act as a close approximation, allowing Monte Carlo generated values to be used in tests for value at risk (Lemmer, 1980). After the random values have been generated they are all then multiplied by the value of the portfolio, with the results sorted into ascending order from smallest to largest, and the percentile value at the chosen significance level is the value at risk. Monte Carlo simulation is essentially exactly the same as the historical simulation method except that historical returns are replaced with randomly generated values.

Detailed steps to calculate the VaR in Excel using the Monte Carlo simulation method are:

*Calculating Monte Carlo simulation VaR in Excel*

1). Note the number of historical interest rate or price change data values used for variance-covariance or historical simulation methods, as the same number of randomly generated numbers will need to be created here. For example, if interest rate changes were in the cells D3:D102 (i.e. one hundred values), then randomly generated values would need to be in e.g. cells J3:J102;

2). Use Excel's 'Data', 'Data Analysis', 'Random Number Generation' option, then fill in the fields with 1 as number of variables, the number of randomly generated values which are required (see above) in the relevant box, select a uniform distribution, and parameters should be between the numbers 0 and 1.

Another way to generate random numbers is to enter the instructions for 12 uniform random numbers minus 6 in every cell requiring a randomly generated value, copying and pasting the following to save time and effort: '=(RAND()+RAND()+RAND()+RAND()+RAND()+RAND()+RAND()+RAND()+RAND()+RAND()+RAND()+RAND()-6)'. This formula approximates a normal distribution as it is symmetric and the sum of twelve uniformly distributed random numbers between 0 and 1 has a mean of 6 and a standard deviation of 1, and subtracting six from this gives a mean of 0 and standard deviation of 1 like a normal distribution;

3) Add a new column in Excel which multiplies each randomly generated number by the overall value of the portfolio;

4). Note where the 'randomly generated number multiplied by portfolio value' data values begin and end in the Excel cells, for example if the first value is in cell K3 and the last in K102 the data range would be 'K3:K102'. Next find a blank cell in Excel and enter the relevant formula as follows: '=PERCENTILE(K3:K102,0.05)' where 'K3:K102' is the range of 'returns multiplied by portfolio value' data values, and 0.05 is the percentage margin of error in the VaR test, e.g. 95% confidence level = 5% or 0.05 margin of error. This gives the relevant value at risk using the Monte Carlo method.

## 3.5 Comparison of VaR Methods

Each of the three methods to calculate value at risk have their own strengths and weakness. The variance-covariance method is based around the volatility of historic returns, and if this is relatively constant and predictable over time then the variance-covariance prediction may be highly accurate. However, the method is based on a normal distribution of returns (symmetrical with zero skewness, and with kurtosis of 3) and assumes that values take a form resembling the following diagram:

# Normal distribution

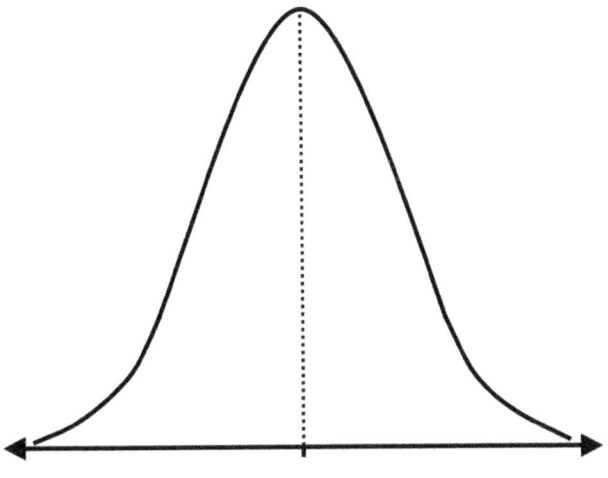

If the return distribution doesn't follow the bell curve pattern as shown with this normal distribution then the variance-covariance method may be inaccurate, and it's useful to plot data returns as a histogram to compare with the bell curve shape. A normality test using statistical software can also be performed, and if the 5% critical value from statistical tables is exceeded then the distribution isn't normal. Another flaw with the variance-covariance method is that it doesn't account for non-linear assets, and option assets where values can take on different forms won't be properly accounted for in the model.

The historical simulation method is based on historical return levels, and if they're constant and predictable over time then the method's estimations may be accurate. One bonus of the approach is that it doesn't require a normal distribution unlike the variance-covariance method. However, the historical simulation is based on only one factor, past values, and if these are radically different to the present then all of its future predictions may be off.

Monte Carlo simulation has two major advantages over the other two methods which may make it the superior value at risk measure, and it does not require a normal distribution in data values as it approximates one itself, nor does it need future data values to bear some resemblance to historical values. However, as it is based entirely on random data values the Monte Carlo method is never likely to be completely accurate.

## 3.6 Square Root of Time Rule

The square root of time rule, or 'root-T' rule for short, allows short-run value at risk (VaR) results to be turned into long-run VaR predictions. For example, a 1 day VaR result using daily sample data could be transformed into a 100 day VaR prediction, or the method could turn a value at risk found using monthly interest rate changes into a value at risk estimation for a year as a whole. The rule simply multiplies the original VaR result value by the square root (root) of the time (T) period desired, and therefore to turn a 1 month result into a 12 month or annual result the monthly VaR is multiplied by $\sqrt{12}$. For example, if the monthly VaR was £10.3 million:

$$\text{Annual VaR, VaR}_{12} = \text{Monthly VaR} * \text{Root-T}$$
$$\text{VaR}_{12} = 10.3 * \sqrt{12}$$
$$\text{VaR}_{12} = £35.68 \text{ million}$$

With a monthly value at risk of £10.3 million the annual 12 month value at risk, $\text{VaR}_{12}$, would be £35.68 million.

However, in order to use the root-T rule and transform monthly value at risk into annual value at risk certain conditions must be met, and factor changes must be identically and independently distributed (i.i.d.) or the square root of time rule won't apply (Cuthbertson and Nitzsche, 2001). The i.i.d. assumption won't hold if the range of values used to calculate the VaR are correlated with each other either positively (a trend) or negatively (mean reversion), violating the independent condition, or if they have a different probability distribution, which violates the identically distributed condition.

## *Autocorrelation test*

Autocorrelation or serial correlation in the data, where there is correlation between a variable and itself over time, is one common way the i.i.d. assumption can be violated. Regression analysis with statistical software can identify the Durbin-Watson (DW) autocorrelation statistic, which will be somewhere between 0 and 4, to reveal whether or not data values are affected by serial correlation. If the DW value is approximately 0 there is perfect positive autocorrelation in the data, and when the level of a factor increases the data values that follow soon after it over time will also increase. If the DW value is approximately 4 then perfect negative autocorrelation exists, and when the level of a factor increases the data value which follows after will exhibit the opposite trend and decrease. And if DW is approximately 2 there's no autocorrelation in the data values. However, when the DW is between 0 and 2, or between 2 and 4, a more detailed test process is required.

First, the number of variable factors or parameters in the model is noted, and this number gives the 'K' value. For example, if interest rate changes (a proxy for bond returns) were the only variable in a model then K =1. Next the number of data observations is noted as the sample size. For example if there were 101 interest rate value observations used to give 100 interest rate change values used for the value at risk calculation, then the sample size number (N) for the DW test would be 100. As with most statistical tests a confidence level must also be decided, and the strictest 99% confidence level (only 1% margin of error or significance level) may be best here. While a greater margin of error (e.g. 5%, for a 95% confidence level) may be useful for a value at risk test, to avoid losing track of the most likely outcome just to take account of very rare occurrences, the purpose of this autocorrelation test is to be sure that the i.i.d. condition holds so the highest 99% confidence level is advised.

With a number of parameters (K), sample size (N), and confidence level the DW test can proceed, and the process compares the calculated DW test result with upper and lower bound critical values from statistical tables. For example, the DW regression result may be 1.8, and with one variable (K = 1), a sample size number of 100, and 99% confidence level (1% or 0.01 significance level) the DW statistical tables give the following critical 'd' values, where du is the upper bound and dl the lower bound:

K = 1; N = 100; Significance level = 1%, 0.01;
dl = 1.52; du = 1.56; DW = 1.8

The DW value from the regression is compared with these dl and du values to assess for autocorrelation:

0 to dl = Positive autocorrelation;
dl to du = Autocorrelation unlikely, but some risk;
du to 4–du = No autocorrelation;
4–du to 4–dl = Autocorrelation unlikely, some risk;
4–dl to 4 = Negative autocorrelation

Not all of the possible outcomes give a clear answer one way or the other, but here the DW = 1.8 test result gives the 'du to 4–du = no autocorrelation' result, as du = 1.56 and 4-du = 2.44, and therefore there is no autocorrelation in the sample data. This supports the i.i.d. criteria of independence in the data, and enables the square root of time rule.

## *Unit root test*

Another issue which can violate the i.i.d. requirement is data which is stationary or mean-reverting, and which reverts back to and stays around a certain level or range over time, a condition which may exist in some prices or returns. This would violate the independence requirement as over time an individual data value would be determined by the mean of all values, instead of being independent and following a 'random walk'. Wu and Zhang (1996) examined interest rates across OECD countries and they find that interest rates are not stationary and predictable in the short-term, and they instead have what is known as a 'unit root' where shocks change the range of future values, but in the long-run and after a period of several years the effect passes and the data reverts to being stationary.

In order to test for a unit root in data values, which would support the i.i.d. conditions required to use the square root of time rule and turn monthly VaR into annual VaR, a Dickey-Fuller unit root test can be performed with statistical software. The augmented Dickey-Fuller (ADF) test result can then be compared to those expected from statistical tables, at the chosen significance level. All results should be negative numbers but if the ADF result is a smaller negative number than the critical value from the statistical table, then the null hypothesis of a unit root is supported and the i.i.d. conditions along with it (Fuller, 1976).

When looking at Dickey-Fuller statistical tables there are usually two different sets of critical values, one which allows for a trend in data values and one which doesn't. Using the set which expects a trend in the data means the critical value will be a larger negative number, such as -3.5 instead of -2.93 for a sample size of 50 and a 5%

significance level, and it will harder and require more evidence to reject the idea of a unit root. Time series data will often have some trends in the data, whether prices, returns or interest rates, and therefore it can be useful to select the Dickey-Fuller test which accounts for a trend. However, a more direct way to account for trends is to simply include lags in variables in the regression, and if this method is chosen then the no trend test should be used as a possible trend has already been accounted for with the lags.

A sample size of 500 data values using the strictest 99% confidence level for a 1% (0.01) significance level gives the following critical value:

Sample size, $N = 500$; Significance level = 1%, 0.01; Critical value = -3.44

If the ADF result calculated with statistical software for the 500 data values was a smaller negative number than the -3.44 value (e.g. -1) then a unit root is present and the root-T conditions met. But if the ADF result was a greater negative number than -3.44 (e.g. -8.4) then the data is instead stationary to violate the i.i.d. conditions needed for the square root of time rule, and the rule can't be used for the data sample.

# 4 Exponentially Weighted Moving Average

## 4.1 Time-Varying Volatility Analysis

While the value at risk measure can give an indication of how much value could be lost from an investor's portfolio in a worst case scenario, a more precise and direct way for an investor to cover against risk is to try to predict price or interest changes. If this information was known then an investor may be able to take direct pre-emptive action to protect against the negative effects of return changes, instead of only preparing to react after problems occur.

An exponentially weighted moving average (EWMA) estimates a range of possible future price or interest rate changes, and it calculates future factor change variance (volatility or standard deviation squared) by replacing the normal equally weighted factor changes with a method that gives more recent changes an exponentially increasing weight. This is because the more recent return volatility is considered to be more representative of what to expect in the future than return volatility which occurred in the distant past. Taking the square root of the EWMA variance predictions can give an indication of potential volatility in future price or interest rate changes and returns, and with this some estimations can be made for future price or yield changes to facilitate financial risk management.

Calculation of the EWMA variance of future price or interest rate returns is quite complicated, and it's easier to perform if taken in steps. The first formula required to find the exponentially weighted moving average is:

EWMA variance for observation n, $\sigma_n^2 = \sum(w_i * r_{n-i}^2)$

This formula states that the variance ($\sigma^2$, standard deviation or volatility, $\sigma$, squared) of observation number 'n' ($\sigma_n^2$), equals the sum ($\sum$) of all exponentially weighted ($w_i$) previous returns squared ($r_{n-i}^2$). Note that volatility and returns are both squared to make positive and negative returns comparable, and to prevent them cancelling each other out to make it appear that volatility is lower than it really is. Weightings, $w_i$, are determined by the formula:

Exponential weightings, $w_i = (1 - \lambda) * \lambda^i$

$\lambda$ is a sensitivity factor showing the responsiveness of variance to factor changes (i.e. how fluctuations in price or interest rate changes effect price or interest rate change variance fluctuations), and $\lambda^i$ is the sensitivity factor discounted by the exponential weighting. The coefficient of sensitivity factor $\lambda$ has been calculated at 0.94 (94%) by the respected RiskMetrics group and this value will be used here. Combining the former two formulas into a third removes the 'i' representing a range of possible values, using the last observation's EWMA value to give a prediction without constant reweighting (Hull, 2009):

$$\text{EWMA variance for observation n, } \sigma_n^2$$
$$= \lambda * \sigma_{n-1}^2 + (1 - \lambda) * r_{n-1}^2$$

This EWMA formula shows that price or interest rate change variance is decided by the previous observation's variance and squared return after accounting for factor sensitivity, where n-1 is the previous observation to that to be estimated, observation n. With the three formulas the EWMA predicted future factor variance can be found, and with it an estimation of future price or interest change volatility to facilitate risk management.

Calculating the EWMA variance in Excel, using the value $\lambda - 0.94$, involves the following steps:

### _Calculating EWMA variance in Excel_

1). Collect interest rate or price data from DataStream and download it into Excel in column B;

2). Create a new column in Excel which divides each and every interest rate data or price value by 100 to turn them into decimal percentage form. For example, if there were fifty-one data values in column B from cells B10 to B60 then in cell C10 type '=B10/100', then move the cursor to the bottom right of cell C10 and click the small '+' symbol to apply the changes to the entire column;

3). Create a new column in Excel which gives changes in data values to reveal the returns. For example, if using non-continuously compounded price data and the price decimal percentage values were in cells C10:C60, then in cell D11 type '=(C11-C10)/C10', and apply this pattern to the D column. With continuously compounded price data the formula would instead be '=LN(C11/C10)', and with interest rate data the formula for column D would be '=C11-C10' and subtraction is used in place of relative changes as the interest rate values matter not just the trend;

4). Square all returns in a new column, and if the return values were in column D in D11:D60 then in cell E11 type '=D11^2' and apply this to the entire E column;

5). Create a new column for the exponential weightings, and if the squared returns were in column E from E11:E60 the new column for weightings would be in column F. Next to the final squared return cell, e.g. next to E60 in F60, type '=(1-0.94)*0.94^0'. This represents the formula for weightings, '$w_i = (1 - \lambda) * \lambda^i$', where the most recent return has the value $i = 0$ in its weighting and doesn't need to be discounted in the EWMA variance formula. In the cell directly above in e.g. F59, next to the second last squared return cell, enter '=F60*0.94' to see the weighting for the second last squared have i = 1, to be discounted with an exponential weighting. Next move the cursor to the bottom right of the cell (e.g. F59) to make the '+' sign appear, and drag the highlighter bars up until every cell requiring a weighting above (e.g. F11:F59) is selected. This ensures all of the cells have the correct exponential weighting, and cell F58 will have 'F59*0.94' for the effect of i = 2, cell F57 the effect of i = 3 etc.;

6). Add a new column (G) multiplying the exponential weightings column (F) with the price or interest rate changes (returns) squared column (E). For example, if the returns squared were in cells E11:E60 and the weightings in cells F11:F60, then in cell G11 enter '=E11*F11' and apply this to the entire G column, G11:G60;

7). In an empty cell, such as H60 for example, total all the G column values using the format '=SUM(G11:G60)'. This gives EWMA formula: '$\sigma_n^2 = \sum(w_i * r_{n-i}^2)$'. Then in an empty cell such as H61 the EWMA variance for the next time period can be found in Excel by entering the formula '=(0.94*H60)+(0.06*E60)' which is EWMA formula: '$\sigma_n^2 = \lambda * \sigma_{n-1}^2 + (1 - \lambda) * r_{n-1}^2$'. 0.06 is $(1 - \lambda)$, E60 is has the most recent squared returns value, $r_{n-1}^2$;

8). The square root of the EWMA value in e.g. H61 using '=SQRT(H61)' gives the next return volatility.

The estimation of the return volatility for the next period shows the possible change in return, which will always have the potential to be up (+) or down (−). For example if the EWMA variance calculation gave 0.000004 the volatility is 0.002, which is ± 0.002 (0.2%) meaning the return may go up 0.2% or down 0.2% next period.

### *Assessment of EWMA*

By giving a range of possible volatility results the EWMA measure serves several purposes at once, and the downside estimation can serve as a value at risk (VaR) type measure, while the upside prediction also shows an asset holder the highest returns they may gain. EWMA advantages are that it only requires the last period's variance and returns to calculate, unlike the variance-covariance and historical VaR measures which require a long history of observations, and unlike the Monte Carlo VaR measure the EWMA is based on empirical evidence not a random distribution and random chance.

However, there are drawbacks to the EWMA measure. As the EWMA requires the last observed return it can only be used accurately for one period ahead, similar to value at risk if the square root of time rule can't be applied. Also, EWMA estimations can't be trusted until they have first been backtested, which is the subject of the next section.

## 4.2 Backtesting

After the EWMA values have been calculated they need to be backtested, to be sure that the results found are reliable and trustworthy for the data sample being used. The backtest multiplies each EWMA prediction by the one-tailed (i.e. one-sided, + or −) normal distribution critical value (1.65 for 5% significance level and 5% margin of error), and this is then compared with the value of the actual empirical price or yield changes. At the 5% significance level no more than 5% of the actual empirical changes should be below '-1.65 * EWMA estimation volatility', and no more than 5% of the actual changes should be above '1.65 * EWMA prediction volatility' (Cuthbertson and Nitzsche, 2001). The backtest should involve a large number of data values for robustness, and the steps to perform the backtest in Excel are as follows:

### *Backtesting EWMA estimations in Excel*

1). Count back 10, 20, 50, or 100 etc. returns squared values from the end of the relevant column in Excel, depending on the data sample size used. For example, with 500 returns squared values in column E in cells E11: E510, count back 100 cells to cell E411 for a backtest of 100 observations in E411:E510;

2). Start the exponential weighting process detailed in section 4.1, in new column I, starting from the time just before where the backtest period begins (i.e. I410 here), and apply the weightings for every cell back to the start of the sample (i.e. I11:I410 here);

3). Create a new column J in Excel which multiplies weightings (I) and returns squared (E) columns;

4). In the K cell to the right of the final J cell just before the backtest begins, i.e. cell K410 to the right of J410 here, calculate the '$\sigma_n^2 = \sum(w_i * r_{n-i}^2)$' value, as a starting point for the EWMA;

5). Apply the '$\sigma_n^2 = \lambda * \sigma_{n-1}^2 + (1 - \lambda) * r_{n-1}^2$' formula as explained above to all of the backtest target cells, e.g. K411:K510 here, to give the EWMA variance;

6). Take the square root of the EWMA variance for all backtested cells in new column L, to calculate estimated volatility by month in e.g. cells L411:L510;

7). Create a new column M in Excel which multiplies backtested volatility values (column L) by -1.65 (negative 1.65) in e.g. cells M411:M510, for the normal distribution test lower boundary;

8). Create a new column N which subtracts the actual yield changes (column C) from the EWMA volatility multiplied by -1.65 (column M) for the backtest period;

9). Create a new column O in Excel and 'Copy', 'Paste Special', 'Paste values' for the differences found in 8) for the backtest period. Sort the data into descending order, and examine the number of values which are positive. If the percentage of the total backtest sample is more than 5% (e.g. more than 5 if backtest size was 100 observations, or more than 1 if backtest sample was 20, then the backtest is failed and the EWMA estimations are unreliable. If 5% or less then the backtest is halfway to being passed at the 95% confidence level (5% margin of error);

10) Repeat steps 7) to 9) using 1.65 (positive 1.65) in place of -1.65 used earlier. This gives the normal distribution upper test boundary. Sort the new subtraction differences into ascending order this time, and examine the number of values which are negative. If the percentage is more than 5% of the total backtest sample size then the test is failed and EWMA can't be trusted with the sample. But if 5% or less, and the percentage found in step 9) was also 5% or less, then the backtest is passed and EWMA is reliable and can be used.

# Note that the method used in steps 7) to 10) is based on a normal distribution. If the data sample is not normally distributed an alternative is to run through the steps using the EWMA volatility values directly, multiplying by -1 and 1 instead of -1.65 and 1.65. There won't be a percentage benchmark to test the results against but general EWMA accuracy can be determined and assessed.

# 5 Orange County 1994 Bankruptcy Case

## 5.1 Background to Orange County Failure

The 1994 bankruptcy of Orange County, California is an interesting real life case study with which to further investigate financial risk management. In December of 1994 Orange County filed for bankruptcy and ultimately reported a loss of $1.64 billion, at the time the largest municipal failure in US history. Although it has since been exceeded in scale in the US by the municipal failures of Jefferson County, Alabama in 2011 and Detroit, Michigan in 2013, the Orange County case retains significant interest due to the cause of the bankruptcy, which was taking risky positions in financial markets without a risk management strategy which covered against interest rate risk.

Robert Citron, long-time treasurer and tax collector of Orange County in 1994, was in a desperate position after local government's tax allocations were cut by the state, and he needed a way to raise income for the county without raising taxes which would alienate the local electorate. Citron embarked on a risky strategy to raise income by borrowing heavily to invest in bond securities which would gain value if interest rates fell, as US interest rates had been following a general downward trend (The Public Policy Institute of California, 1998). This strategy also took advantage of natural uneven bond convexity, noted earlier, where increases in yields reduce price and value less than an equivalent yield decrease raises price.

The chosen investment portfolio for the Orange County Investment Pool (OCIP) mostly consisted of fixed income securities and structured notes, with additional funds obtained with the issuing of reverse repurchase agreements, a debt where a security is bought with the agreement to sell it on later for a higher price. This reverse repurchase agreements debt ensured a highly leveraged and risky position for Orange County's books.

An examination of empirical evidence on historical portfolio performance explains Citron's choice of assets. Asness (1996) notes that a levered portfolio of stocks and bonds outperformed an unlevered portfolio of 100% equities over the years 1926-1993. Overall a levered portfolio offered higher total returns than the unlevered comparison, with the same long-term consistency, and comparable standard deviation and worst case scenario outcomes. Based on this information Bob Citron's choice of investment appeared wise, and it was successful at first as US interest rates fell steadily over the years 1989-93 to see the portfolio rise in value.

February 1994 saw the beginning of a series of sharp rises in US interest rates as the Federal Reserve looked to tighten credit to reduce the threat of inflation and prevent the US economy from overheating. The constant maturity treasury rate rose from 3.45% in February 1994 to 7.14% in December 1994 (from 3.61% a year before in December 1993). These yield rises caused Orange County's portfolio to plummet in value, and some predicted Citron would lead the county to bankruptcy. John Moorlach was one dissenting voice and he ran for public office against Citron in the June 1994 Orange County Treasurer local election, opposing the reckless investments Citron had made with billions of dollars of public money. But Bob Citron won the public vote and remained in control of the Orange County Investment Pool for the rest of 1994.

In an attempt to reclaim funds lost from rising interest rates and secure the high returns required for his county Bob Citron went on to borrow further, doubling down on the investment strategy of betting on falling interest rates and a yield trend reversal. But the reversal didn't come in time and when Citron couldn't keep up with margin payments on the debt funds borrowed in the repo market, due to low returns from a bad investment strategy, the game was up. Orange County was unable to sell portfolio assets seen by other investors as too risky, and when creditors moved in to seize assets as collateral in December 1994 the county declared bankruptcy.

## 5.2 Balance Sheet and Risk at Bankruptcy

The balance sheet of Orange County on 1st December 1994 was as follows:

### ASSETS ($): 20.5 billion

Structures Notes (38%)
Inverse floating-rate notes (26.1%): **5.4 billion**
Others (dual index notes (0.7%), floating-rate notes (2.9%), index-amortizing notes (8.3%)): **2.4 billion**

Fixed-income securities (57.7%): **11.9 billion**

Cash (3.2%): **0.6 billion**

Collateralized mortgage obligations (1.1%): **0.2 billion**

### LIABILITIES ($): 20.5 billion

Reverse repurchase agreements (63.2%): **13 billion**

Investor equity (36.8%): **7.5 billion**

## *Leverage and risk exposure*

The balance sheet for Orange County in December 1994 can be used to find the county's risk exposure and leverage at the time of their bankruptcy declaration:

$$\text{Leverage} = \text{Total liabilities} / \text{Non-debt liabilities}$$
$$\text{Leverage} = \text{Total liabilities} / \text{Investor equity}$$
$$\text{Leverage} = 20.5 / 7.5$$
$$\text{Leverage} = 2.7$$

In December 1994 Orange County's leverage was roughly 2.7, almost three times the unleveraged factor of 1. Reverse repos debt of $13 billion dwarfed equity of $7.5 billion, which makes Robert Citron's securities strategy look less like a well thought out investment plan based on the historical benefits of combining debt with equity, and more like a naive gamble on the potentially lucrative benefits of reverse repurchase agreements. The interest rate risk exposure linked with the 2.7 leverage factor, combined with the rising trend in interest rates at the time, suggests that the value of Orange County's securities portfolio may have been likely to fall even lower, and the decision to declare bankruptcy and avoid further losses may have been the best move. An examination of the county's duration and risk sensitivity can offer further insight into this area.

## _Duration and effective duration_

Orange County's (Macaulay) duration at the time of the bankruptcy in December 1994 is known to have been 2.74, as most of the securities in the portfolio had a maturity below five years. This may explain the decision to declare bankruptcy, as Orange County was in urgent need of funds but most of their portfolio's cash flows wouldn't be received for years. However, the flaws of duration include it not being able to fully represent assets with embedded options or which relate to real estate, both of which are a part of the portfolio here.

The effective duration measure is one way to overcome flaws with duration, and it can reveal the interest rate sensitivity and predict portfolio price changes after changes in interest rates more directly. But the leveraged nature of the Orange County portfolio with its debt payments may make it hard to predict the effect of various yield changes on price, preventing the effective duration calculation. The more general version of effective duration can be used however, and multiplying portfolio duration of 2.74 years by the exposure to interest rate risk and leverage factor of 2.7 calculated earlier gives effective duration:

Effective duration = Duration * Leverage
Effective duration = 2.74 * 2.7

Effective duration = 7.4 years

When the Orange County securities portfolio leverage is taken into account the situation looks bleak. Most of the portfolio value would not be received in cash payments for over 7 years, yet debt repayments were owed on a continuous basis and the portfolio's debt could be called in at any time. Even if interest rates were to have fallen suddenly, as Orange County's leadership would have hoped, this would also have the effect of further increasing duration as lower interest rates would reduce the discounting rate of distant future cash flows, to ensure that most of the portfolio's value would only be received long into the future. This supports the idea that Orange County was right to declare bankruptcy at the time they did, as waiting for the cash flows they required to materialize may have appeared likely to be a losing proposition.

## *Modified duration and risk sensitivity*

Modified duration is calculated using duration and the yield to maturity (YTM), and it can be used to assess the risk sensitivity of portfolio prices to interest rate changes. It can be used to assess whether Orange County's portfolio loss of $1.64 billion could have been predicted following the yield changes in 1994, and if it could then Orange County may have been able to protect their portfolio with effective risk management before the yield changes occurred.

Although benchmark interest rates were lower the constant maturity 1 year treasury rate may be a more accurate and applicable YTM measure to account for the reverse repos debt securities in the portfolio. The 1994 yield changes saw the constant maturity treasury 1 year yield rate change from 3.61% in December 1993 to 7.14% in December 1994, a change of roughly 3.5% (Mortgage-X.com, 2014). The duration level of 2.74 can be used for the modified duration calculation, and although this was the December 1994 level and duration may have been different a year earlier this is the only value available and will have to do as a proxy. Annual interest payments are assumed (m = 1). December 1993 modified duration was:

$$\text{Modified duration } (D_M) = \text{Duration} / (1 + i / m)$$
$$D_M = 2.74 / (1 + 0.0361 / 1)$$
$$D_M = 2.645$$

This modified duration value can then be used to predict the effect of 1994 interest changes on portfolio value, with a portfolio price of $20.5 billion:

$$D_M \text{ price change estimate: } \Delta P = -D_M * \%\Delta Y * \text{Bond price}$$
$$D_M \text{ price change estimate: } \Delta P = -2.645 * 0.035 * 20.5$$
$$D_M \text{ estimated price change: } \Delta P = \$-1.898 \text{ billion}$$

Modified duration estimates that Orange County's portfolio would lose $1.898 billion in value following the 3.5% 1994 yield changes, an overestimate compared to the actual loss Orange County faced of $1.64 billion.

The disparity between the predicted loss and actual loss may be partly explained by the embedded option assets (structured notes) and real estate (reverse repurchase agreements) in the portfolio, which the duration value may not take into account, or perhaps the duration or yield rate values chosen for the formula did not represent exactly what Orange County faced over 1994. But the main cause of the disparity may be the convexity of the bonds in the portfolio, and it has been noted that with yield falls modified duration will underestimate price increases and value gains, and with yield rises modified duration will overestimate price decreases and value losses. Convexity and convexity's estimate of the effect interest changes have on portfolio price changes could be added to the analysis, but unfortunately a convexity value for Orange County's 1994 portfolio is unavailable, as is detailed cash flow information to allow for it to be calculated.

The $(1.898 / 1.64) - 1 = 15.7\%$ overestimate is not that large however, and if the convexity estimation of interest rate changes on portfolio price was included it's reasonable to assume that the estimated loss here could be close to the actual loss of $1.64 billion. This suggests the modified duration measure could be used to predict what could have happened after December 1994 if Orange County hadn't faced financial problems. In December 1994 the constant maturity treasury 1 year yield rate was 7.14%, for the modified duration value:

$$\text{Modified duration } (D_M) = \text{Duration} / (1 + i / m)$$
$$D_M = 2.74 / (1 + 0.0714 / 1)$$
$$D_M = 2.557$$

The modified duration estimate for the portfolio price change can then be used to predict the effect of an increase in yield rate of 0.5%, to assess what might have happened if Orange County had managed to hold out and avoid financial failure for another month. The 0.5% yield increase amount had already occurred in a previous month in 1994 and could easily have happened the next month in January 1995, if the trend at the time of interest rate increases had continued.

$$D_M \text{ price change estimate: } \Delta P = -D_M * \%\Delta Y * \text{Bond price}$$
$$D_M \text{ price change estimate: } \Delta P = -2.557 * 0.005 * 20.5$$
$$D_M \text{ price change estimate: } \Delta P = \$-0.262 \text{ billion}$$

If yield rates had increased by 0.5% in January 1995, which was not too unreasonable an assumption at the time following what had recently occurred in 1994, then Orange County stood to lose another $0.262 billion. Avoiding this risk is likely to have been a driving factor in the bankruptcy declaration.

## *Conclusion*

The above analysis for leverage, duration, effective duration, and modified duration's estimate of portfolio price falls after interest rate increases suggests that the Orange County portfolio had a high risk exposure in December 1994, at the time of the bankruptcy declaration. Bearing in mind that risk exposure had caused them nothing but ever increasing financial loss during 1994 to the scale of billions of dollars, the decision of Orange County to finally cut their losses at the end on the year and give up on their portfolio of assets invested in decreasing interest rates may have been a smart move.

However, the risk exposure Orange County held was already well known, and Bob Citron had deliberately put the county into that position throughout 1994 as he mistakenly thought the risk would work in his favour. The most important issue is not that there was risk but whether the interest rate increases and trends in 1994 could have been predicted, and the risk managed. This is the focus of the next section.

# 6 Risk Management for Orange County

## 6.1 Value at Risk for Orange County

The value at risk measure can give an insight into whether Orange County could have known predicted changes in their portfolio value, and undertook risk management in response. A comparison between the value at risk estimations using the variance-covariance, historical simulation, and Monte Carlo simulation methods and the actual portfolio loss over 1994 can suggest which method was the most accurate, and which was likely to be most accurate beyond December 1994 to predict what may have happened if Orange County hadn't declared bankruptcy. And as the accuracy of the variance-covariance method is based around the predictability of return volatility, the historical simulation method on return level predictability, and the Monte Carlo method based upon random chance, a comparison between the three will also give insight into whether the 1994 changes in returns (i.e. interest rate and yield changes) could have been predicted. If they could then a different outcome may have been possible.

Before the value at risk methods can be used yield rate data for the period is required, and yield rate changes must be calculated to act as a direct representation for changes in the value of Orange County's bond portfolio. DataStream is one source for this, and the data values chosen were:

5 year yields p.a. on current US treasury issues
Monthly data, December 1952 to December 1994

5 year yields per annum (p.a.) are used in place of the 1 year constant maturity treasury rate used for modified duration, as the analysis here is concerned with longer term trends and patterns in the data and longer run yields are more relevant. Monthly data was used as interest rate changes are made monthly by the Federal Reserve. 505 data values were selected ending in December 1994 when Orange County went bankrupt and going back to December 1952, and turning interest rate values into interest rate changes from month to month (for bond portfolio returns) removes the first value, leaving 504 values over 42 full years from January 1953 to December 1994. 500+ data values is enough to assess interest rate volatility and return levels without being misled by temporary trends, while the inclusion of 42 full years in place of partial years removes the risk that calendar effects for certain months could distort results.

## *Variance-covariance method*

The 5 year yields per annum monthly data values were turned into yield changes which will act as a proxy for bond returns, and then their volatility (standard deviation) was calculated using the method outlined in section 3.2, for a value of 0.0040365. This is then multiplied by the weighting for bonds relative to cash in the assets of the portfolio to give the portfolio volatility, and this comes to (5.4+2.4+11.9+0.2) / 20.5 = 19.9/20.5 = 0.97073.

Portfolio volatility = Bond volatility * Weight of bonds in portfolio
Portfolio volatility = 0.0040365 * 0.97073
Portfolio volatility = 0.00391835

This result is multiplied by the value of the Orange County portfolio in December 1994, $20.5 billion, and the critical value (CV) at the 95% confidence level or 5% significance level, 1.65, for the variance-covariance VaR:

VaR = Portfolio value * Portfolio volatility * CV
VaR = 20.5 * 0.00391835 * 1.65
VaR = $0.132538 billion

The variance-covariance method predicts that the monthly value at risk for Orange County in December

1994 was $0.132538 billion, and that there was a 95% chance that the total loss over the next month would be no higher than $0.132528 billion.

## *Historical simulation method*

5 year yields monthly data is also used for the historical simulation method, and yield changes month to month are multiplied by the value of the portfolio, $20.5 billion, as detailed in section 3.3. This gives a series of data values and the value at the 5% percentile after sorting them in ascending order gives the 95% confidence level value at risk:

VaR = Significance level percentile value for sorted values
of (Portfolio value * Returns)
VaR = $0.12177 billion

Monthly value at risk for December 1994 using the historical simulation method was therefore $0.12177 billion.

## *Monte Carlo simulation method*

The Monte Carlo simulation method doesn't use any yield data at all, and instead generates uniform random numbers between 0 and 1 as explained in section 3.4.

These values are each then multiplied by the value of the Orange County portfolio, $20.5 billion, to give a new series of numbers. Taking the 5% percentile value after the numbers have been sorted into ascending order gives the 95% confidence level Monte Carlo simulation method value at risk:

VaR = Significance level percentile value for sorted values of (Portfolio value * Randomly generated values)
VaR = $0.361143 billion

Although the Monte Carlo simulation VaR result will be different every time as it is based on random numbers, the monthly VaR for December 1994 calculated here is $0.361143 billion. Running through the Monte Carlo simulation method many times again to test the robustness of this result gave different values but they were always within the $0.30 billion to $0.39 billion range, which suggests the original result is representative of what to expect from the method.

## *Comparison of the 3 VaR methods and results*

The Monte Carlo monthly VaR result of $0.36 billion is significantly larger than the variance-covariance VaR result of $0.13 billion, and the historical simulation result of $0.12 billion. But there's no way to know for sure which of these predictions was the most accurate as they are all for December 1994, the month Orange County declared bankruptcy to avoid suffering further losses, and at this time there was no longer a portfolio with value to lose. However, the variance-covariance method is based on a normal distribution in the data, which may not hold here.

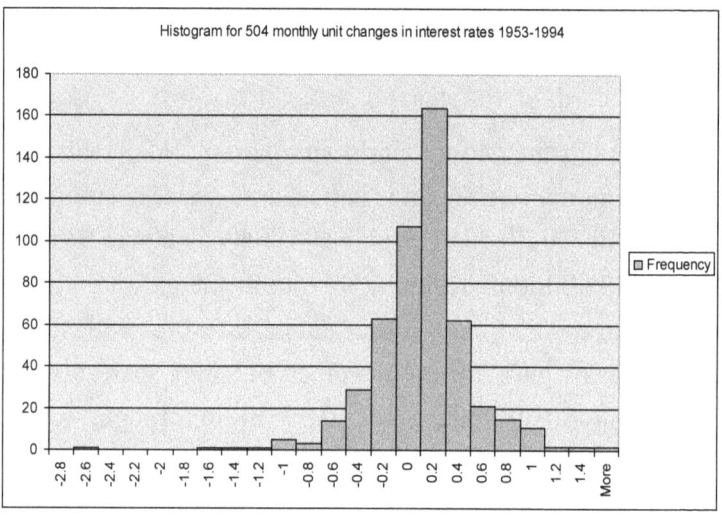

This diagram is a histogram of monthly yield changes using 5 year yields per annum 1953-94 data. The skewness and peakedness suggest the data doesn't follow a normal distribution like the diagram in section 3.5. A Jarque-Bera (JB) chi-squared normality test using statistical software confirms that the 1953-94 data doesn't follow a normal distribution, as the calculated JB result exceeds the chi-squared critical value found from statistical tables, to reject the null hypothesis of normality:

Sample size, N = 504; Significance level = 5%, 0.05;
Chi-squared critical value = 5.99; JB result = 301.7

The non-normal distribution here violates variance-covariance method assumptions and its requirements. Another problem with the accuracy of the method here is the embedded options (structured notes) in Orange County's portfolio, and the variance-covariance analysis can't adequately account for these.

The square root of time rule, or 'root-T' rule, allows monthly VaR values to be turned into longer period VaR values by multiplying by the square root of the VaR time period required. This means that the calculated December 1994 month VaR results can be turned into annual predictions for all of 1994, to see which method was actually the most accurate over the year. The monthly predictions for December 1994, which could never be tested as Orange County declared bankruptcy that month, were as follows:

Variance-covariance: VaR = $0.132538 billion
Historical simulation: VaR = $0.12177 billion
Monte Carlo simulation: VaR = $0.361143 billion

And the 1 month VaR numbers can be turned into 12 month values with the root-T rule by multiplying them by the square root of 12 (time in months, T):

Annual VaR, $VaR_{12}$ = Monthly VaR * Root-T
Variance-covariance $VaR_{12}$ = \$0.132538 billion*$\sqrt{12}$
Variance-covariance $VaR_{12}$ = \$0.459125 billion

Historical simulation $VaR_{12}$ = \$0.12177 billion*$\sqrt{12}$
Historical simulation $VaR_{12}$ = \$0.421824 billion

Monte Carlo $VaR_{12}$ = \$0.361143 billion*$\sqrt{12}$
Monte Carlo $VaR_{12}$ = \$1.251036 billion

The variance-covariance method estimates that Orange County would have an annual VaR of \$0.459 billion over the year 1994, the historical simulation method predicts that the annual VaR for 1994 would be \$0.421 billion, and the Monte Carlo simulation approach estimates that the annual VaR at \$1.25 billion. Orange County's actual portfolio loss over 1994 and the period of successive yield rises was \$1.64 billion, and although all of the three different value at risk method's predictions underestimated this, the Monte Carlo method estimation is by far the closest to the facts.

As the random Monte Carlo method appears to be a better predictor for Orange County's 1994 losses than the variance-covariance method based on historical volatility, or the historical simulation method based on historical return levels, it seems that the 1994 portfolio value losses were primarily random and not based on any historical factors. This may suggest that well researched financial risk management may never have been successful, not before the interest rate changes nor at the time of the bankruptcy, and it promotes an excessively risk averse policy where an asset holder would never have taken on the risk which Bob Citron did in the first place. However, as none of the three value at risk methods are close to predicting the actual 1994 loss of \$1.64 billion all of them have their limitations.

Before any definitive conclusions can be drawn from the annual value at risk estimations the square root of time rule's requirements must be met, or the calculations that created the annual values from monthly VaR values can't be used.

## *Square root of time rule requirements*

Use of the square root of time rule to turn monthly VaR values into annual results has certain assumptions, and the inaccuracy of the 1994 annual VaR predictions may be down to these requirements not being met. Section 3.6 explained that data values must be independently and identically distributed (i.i.d.) for the root-T rule to apply, and this can be violated by autocorrelation in the data.

With the strictest 99% confidence level (1% significance level, 0.01) Durbin-Watson autocorrelation test critical values are dl = 1.52, du = 1.56. Regression analysis of the 504 monthly yield changes values, derived from the 5 year yields per annum on current US treasury issues data, gives the following DW statistic:

Durbin-Watson statistic, DW = 1.74
No. of parameters, K = 1; Sample size, N = 504
dl = 1.52; du = 1.56;

And the result of the autocorrelation test is found by comparing the DW value with the dl and du values:

0 to dl = Positive autocorrelation;
dl to du = Autocorrelation unlikely, but some risk;
du to 4–du = No autocorrelation;
4–du to 4–dl = Autocorrelation unlikely, some risk;
4–dl to 4 = Negative autocorrelation

4-du = 2.44 here, and this puts the DW = 1.74 value in the 'du to 4-du = no autocorrelation' range, to support the i.i.d. conditions for the square root of time rule.

Another way that the i.i.d. condition can be violated is if data is stationary or mean-reverting, which also goes against the independence condition. Using a statistical unit root test on interest rate change data reveals the augmented Dicker-Fuller (ADF) result to be -9.006. With the strictest 99% confidence level and 1% significance level, and with 6 period lags to account for trends, the critical value for the 1953-94 yield data from statistical tables is:

Sample size, N = 504; Significance level = 1%, 0.01;
Critical value = -3.446; ADF result = -9.006

As the ADF value of -9.006 is a greater negative number than the critical value of -3.446 the null hypothesis of a unit root is rejected, and there is no unit root in the data. Instead it is stationary and this violates the i.i.d. conditions and invalidates the root-T rule, and the annual value at risk results found above using it.

However, Wu and Zhang (1996) note that although interest rate data may be stationary in the long-run, in short-run periods of a few years evidence suggests that interest rates may exhibit a unit root. Using a sub-sample of the full 1953-94 yield changes can reveal more, and running the unit root test on only 5 years of yield changes from 1990-4 reveals a different trend with a unit root:

Sample size, N = 60; Significance level = 1%, 0.01;
Critical value = -3.557; ADF result = -1.842

The ADF result of -1.842 found with a unit root test is lower than the critical value of -3.557 for a sample size of 60 at the 1% significance level, and the null hypothesis of a unit root and non-stationary data can't be rejected. This would support the i.i.d. assumption and the root-T rule, contradicting the results using the full data sample.

If the full 1953-94 sample of yield changes is examined to look at long-term interest rate trends then the i.i.d. conditions are not met due to stationary data, and the root-T rule can't be used. This means that an accurate annual value at risk can't be found using monthly yield changes, and only monthly VaR values are available. Orange County couldn't know how much of their portfolio value was at risk beyond the next month, and any risk management would therefore have to be done on only a month by month basis, which would be likely to make this task very difficult.

If only the 1990-94 sub-sample of yield changes are used then the data does have a unit root, and it meets the i.i.d. conditions to allow the square root of time rule to be used to predict annual value at risk. But as noted above the unit root would only be temporary and in time interest rates appear to return to a stationary process with all of its problems. And bearing in mind the upward trend in yield rates during 1994, the unit root and lack of mean reversion found in 1990-94 yields would be bad news for Orange County's prospects and income if they hadn't declared bankruptcy in December 1994. Their income and future prospects were directly linked with and depended upon on yield falls and a reversal in the yield trends of the time.

## *Conclusion*

Putting all of the analysis together it seems that all three of the value at risk methods, variance covariance, historical simulation, and Monte Carlo simulation, have their weaknesses. None can be used to accurately predict what actually happened to Orange County in 1994, leaving little confidence that they would be able to predict what would happen in the future to allow risk management. And the square root of time rule which allows monthly interest rate changes to be aggregated for longer value at risk periods appears unusable for Orange County, as interest rates appear to exhibit stationary characteristics which violate the rule's key assumptions. This is another obstacle preventing successful long-run financial risk management. It seems that the value at risk measure wouldn't have helped Orange County much in the 1994 period where they faced financial problems, and other tools are therefore required.

## 6.2 EWMA for Orange County

An exponentially weighted moving average (EWMA) for Orange County's portfolio can reveal if the yield changes which pushed the county to bankruptcy in December 1994 could have been predicted and managed. Using the same 5 year yields per annum 1953-94 data as with the value at risk calculations, the method to calculate the EWMA yield change (return) variance was the same as outlined in section 4.1. The following equations were used where sensitivity factor $\lambda = 0.94$ (94%), $\sigma_{n-1}^2$ is the previous EWMA variance, and $r_{n-1}^2$ is the previous return (yield change) squared:

EWMA variance for observation n, $\sigma_n^2 = \sum(w_i * r_{n-i}^2)$
Exponential weightings, $w_i = (1 - \lambda) * \lambda^i$
EWMA variance for observation n, $\sigma_n^2$
$= \lambda * \sigma_{n-1}^2 + (1 - \lambda) * r_{n-1}^2$

The EWMA variance can be used to estimate the 11 months of yield changes from February to December 1994, the period which led to the bankruptcy at the end of 1994. Taking the square root of the EWMA monthly variance results gives a EWMA prediction for the month's yield volatility or standard deviation, which can be compared with actual yield change to assess EWMA estimations.

First the '$\sigma_n^2 = \sum(w_i * r_{n-i}^2)$' formula was used for the January 1994 value as a starting point, and then the '$\sigma_n^2 = \lambda * \sigma_{n-1}^2 + (1 - \lambda) * r_{n-1}^2$' formula was used to find each month's estimated (E) value from February 1994 onwards:

*Actual (A) and EWMA estimated (E) yield changes*

FEBRUARY: (A) +0.006; (E) $\pm$ 0.002759785
MARCH: (A) +0.0063; (E) $\pm$ 0.003052774
APRIL: (A) +0.0032; (E) $\pm$ 0.003337913
MAY: (A) +0.0012; (E) $\pm$ 0.003329799
JUNE: (A) +0.0017; (E) $\pm$ 0.003241714
JULY: (A) –0.0026; (E) $\pm$ 0.003170424
AUGUST: (A) +0.0008; (E) $\pm$ 0.003139123
SEPTEMBER: (A) +0.0047; (E) $\pm$ 0.003049794
OCTOBER: (A) +0.002; (E) $\pm$ 0.003173101
NOVEMBER: (A) +0.0031; (E) $\pm$ 0.003115198
DECEMBER: (A) +0.0004; (E) $\pm$ 0.003114288

FEB to DEC total: (A) +0.0268; (E) $\pm$ 0.034483914

The EWMA estimate yield changes can be both positive and negative, and the estimates (E) appear relatively accurate as 8 of the 11 actual (A) empirical yield changes from February to December 1994 were within the range the EWMA predicted (only February, March and September were outside the prediction range). Most importantly the total of the actual eleven months yield changes from February to December, +0.0268 (+2.68%), is within the range predicted by the EWMA volatility formula, $\pm$ 0.034483914 ($\pm$ 3.45%).

The EWMA yield volatility estimation is usually larger than the actual volatility, and this suggests it could improve upon the variance-covariance and historical simulation VaR predictions which were based on equally weighted actual data values, and were found to significantly underestimate the VaR and value losses Orange County could face in 1994. But even if an accurate value at risk substitute couldn't be found, if the EWMA measure can predict upper and lower interest rate margins with accuracy it can still facilitate strategies to manage interest rate risk.

## *Backtesting results*

The backtesting method described in section 4.2 was used on the 5 year yields per annum on current US treasury issues 1953-94, and a data sample of 100 values was tested to assess EWMA reliability, starting in September 1986 and ending in December 1994. With a backtest sample size of 100 and 95% confidence level no more than 5 (5%) yield change values were allowed to be above the upper boundary of 1.65 * the EWMA volatility, and no more than 5 (5%) could be below -1.65 * the EWMA volatility. Results were as follows:

No. of values allowed above upper boundary: 5
No. of values allowed below lower boundary: 5
Actual no. values above upper boundary: 5
Actual no. values below lower boundary: 2

These results show that the 1953-94 yield changes passed the EWMA backtest, and the EWMA can be used for this data. However, the backtest tested against a normal distribution, and as noted in section 6.1 the 1953-94 data doesn't follow a normal distribution. But an alternative method, noted at the end of section 4.2, is to run the 100 sample backtest by comparing yield change values with EWMA predictions directly, without multiplying the latter by 1.65 or -1.65 to simulate a normal distribution. The results of this procedure are:

Actual no. values above EWMA predictions: 12
Actual no. values below EWMA predictions: 15

There is no percentage level to assess these results against, but EWMA is 88% accurate (12 out of 100, or 12% inaccurate) for the yield rises which were the cause of Orange County's bankruptcy, and 85% (15 out of 100, or 15% inaccurate) for yield falls.

# 7 Hedging Strategies for Orange County

## 7.1 Hedging Interest Rate Risk

The last section on backtesting confirmed that the EWMA model can predict a general range of yield change values with good accuracy for Orange County. But by late 1994 it was too late for the county to use this information to alter their portfolio and take on opposite positions to hedge interest rate risk and offset value losses, to prepare for the worst case scenario where interest rates rose to the upper boundary predicted by the EWMA volatility. By this time Orange County was in significant debt and its resources went toward meeting debt payments, while its risky assets were unpopular and couldn't be sold to generate additional revenue to fund new portfolio assets. There was little opportunity to stage a recovery even with the EWMA yield volatility information, and all that could be done was to hope for yield falls to reduce the debt.

However, Orange County could have invested their resources into hedging interest rate risk in late 1993 or early 1994, before the damaging yield rises removed the option. But although methods were available at that time to hedge interest rate risk and offset possible financial loss with opposite and equivalent investment positions, as Orange County ultimately required in 1994, investment of resources in such tools would by definition take resources away from those assets which generated profits in the event that interest rates fall. And that was a trend Orange County had benefitted from in the years prior to 1994, and a trend that yield rates followed again in 1995. Successful risk management is therefore not just about reducing risk but balancing risk and reward as efficiently as possible, given limited knowledge of future yield change directions. The next section examines a range of possible hedging instruments which can support this process.

## 7.2 Financial Derivative Instruments

Once an asset holder's circumstances are known a relevant set of investments can be chosen to meet their needs. Orange County's focus was hedging interest rate risk and most financial assets such as simple stocks wouldn't have served any purpose, as they hold no direct correlation to interest rates. But a range of financial derivatives instruments may have supported their goals after using the EWMA to predict a range of possible yield changes.

Futures contracts, where there's an agreement to buy ('long') or sell ('short') an underlying asset at a certain future time at a certain price, are often used to hedge risk. The idea is to create a 'perfect hedge' where the risk associated with one asset is completely eliminated by taking an exactly equal and opposite position in the futures market. However, the strategy is only possible if a futures contract exists which exactly matches the obligation to be hedged, in terms of the asset's nature and delivery terms (Luenberger, 1997). The range of assets Orange County held, which weren't futures contracts, mean that a perfect hedge using a specific set of futures wasn't possible.

One alternative to a perfect hedge was to use interest rate futures to cross hedge interest rate risk. Eurodollar futures can lock in a future interest rate for a 3 month period, and to hedge 1994 interest rate risk 4 consecutive futures could been utilised at the start of the year. The futures quote is 100 minus the futures interest rate and if Orange County sold Eurodollars futures short they could have benefitted from a rise in interest rates, to create end period profits. A certain amount shorted in Eurodollar future contracts could have covered most of the county's losses and hedged interest rate risk (Hull, 2008).

Treasury bill (T-bill) futures could have hedged interest rate risk once Orange County needed to borrow money. Shorting (selling) 4 consecutive 3 month T-bill futures in a cross hedge for loan costs could hedge one year's interest rate risk as T-bills can proxy for interest rates. But the number of T-bills sold must always account for the lower sensitivity of futures prices to yield changes relative to spot prices, due to their shorter maturity (Cuthbertson and Nitzsche, 2001).

There are also non-futures derivatives which could hedge interest rate risk. Swaptions could give the holder the right but not the obligation to perform an interest rate swap at a future time. Orange County had the opportunity to take up a long (buy) position to pay for the right to a certain fixed-rate loan at a set interest rate at a future time. And at that future time the swaption could have been either taken or exercised for savings instead, depending on which was more profitable at the time given the relative level of the market interest rate.

Another interest rate derivative is the interest rate cap, and this could have hedged the risk associated with the floating-rate notes in Orange County's portfolio. For example, if an investor goes long (buy) on a 5 year cap at a 4% rate then if the floating interest rate exceeds 4% at quarterly reset the caplet will be exercised, and cash will be received as profit, at an amount decided by the formula: 'principal * 0.25 * rate difference' (Hull, 2008). The principal is the amount invested, 0.25 represents the quarterly reset (1/4), and the rate difference is the excess of the current floating rate above the caplet rate.

# Bibliography

Asness, C. (1996) Why Not 100% Equities, *The Journal of Portfolio Management*, Vol. 22, No. 2.

Cuthbertson, K. and Nitzsche, D. (2001) *Financial Engineering: Derivatives and Risk Management*, J. Wiley.

Fabozzi, F., Buetow, G. and Johnson, R. (2005) Measuring Interest Rate Risk, *Handbook of Fixed-Income Securities*, 7th edition, New York, McGraw-Hill.

Fooladi, I. and Roberts, G. (2000) Risk Management with Duration Analysis, *Managerial Finance*, Vol. 26, No. 3.

Fuller, W. A. (1976) *Introduction to Statistical Time Series*, New York: John Wiley and Sons.

Hull, J. C. (2008) *Options, Futures and Other Derivatives*, 7th edition, Prentice-Hall.

Hull, J. C. (2009) *Risk Management and Financial Institutions*, 2nd edition, Pearson.

Lemmer, H. (1980) An Estimator for Spread, *Journal of Statistical Computation and Simulation*, Vol. 11, No. 2.

Linsmeier, T. and Pearson, N. (2000) Risk Measurement: An Introduction to Value at Risk, *Financial Analysts Journal*, Vol. 56, No. 2.

Luenberger, D. (1997) *Investment Science*, Oxford University Press.

Mortgage-X Mortgage Information Service (2014) *Constant Maturity Treasury (CMT or TCM) Monthly Historic Data*, Mortgage-X.com
http://mortgage-x.com/general/indexes/cmt_tcm_history.asp?f=m

Public Policy Institute of California (1998) When Government Fails: The Orange County Bankruptcy, a Policy Summary, *The Second Annual California Issues Forum*, Sacramento, California.

Reilly, F. and Brown, K. (2008) *Investment Analysis and Portfolio Management*, 9th edition, South-Western.

Wu, Y. and Zhang, H. (1996) Mean Reversion in Interest Rates: New Evidence form a Panel of OECD Countries, *Journal of Money, Credit and Banking*, Vol. 28, No. 4.

www.ingramcontent.com/pod-product-compliance
Lightning Source LLC
Chambersburg PA
CBHW051338170526
45166CB00002B/863